Born to Travel

ADVENTURES

ADVENTURE is waiting for You

Let's travel around world

Adventure Awaits

travel

TRAVEL IS CALLING

CAN WE JUST SKIP TO THE PART OF MY LIFE WHERE I TRAVEL THE WORLD?

Book

busy traveler

Greetings from AWAY.

AWAY

Discover

whenever you want

HOBBIES

PASSION IS ENERGY.
FEEL THE POWER THAT
COMES FROM FOCUSING ON
WHAT EXCITES YOU.

RELAX AND ENJOY ACTIVITIES

PASSION IS ENERGY.
FEEL THE POWER THAT
COMES FROM FOCUSING ON
WHAT EXCITES YOU.

RELAX AND ENJOY ACTIVITIES

MOTIVATIONAL & ACHIEVEMENTS

Believe in Yourself

Live your dreams, not your fears

You are ENOUGH

⭐⭐⭐⭐⭐⭐⭐⭐⭐⭐

I CAN DO ANYTHING I SET MY MIND TO

just trust yourself

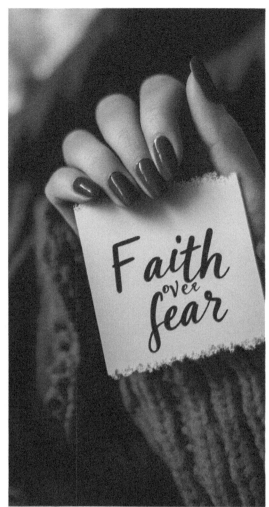

Faith & Spirituality

Thank You

Faith, Hope, Love

Faith

God first.

I AM ONE WITH ALL

Grateful & Blessed

RELATIONSHIP

TRUE love

LOVE WITH Passion

You are my best friend and lover

Work HARD SHOW THEM!

ready **FOR BIGGER** and **BETTER** things

Put YOUR ideas OUT INTO THE WORLD

Surround **YOURSELF** with **POSITIVE PEOPLE**

THIS IS THE SIGN **YOU'VE BEEN** WAITING FOR

THE SECRET to getting ahead is GETTING STARTED

BUILDING MY *empire.*

BUSINESS

SUCCESS *is a decision*

Confident CORE

FUTURE millionaire.

TRUST **THE** *process*

I CAN ACHIEVE ANY GOALS IN BUSINESS

BE THE LIGHT

STRONG Women **MOTIVATE** *inspire empower*

She DREAMS. BELIEVES. ACHIEVES. I AM SHE IS ME.

Minding my **own** *small business*

Style AND GRACE

FOCUSED DETERMINED *unstoppable*

this is us
OUR LIFE. OUR STORY. OUR HOME.

There is no place like home

HOME

HOME -sweet- HOME

Welcome Home

I DESERVE AN AMAZING HOME

this is our *happy place*

YES, MY BFF IS Crazy

Better Together

FRIENDS

World's GREATEST Friends

BEST **friends** FOREVER

FRIENDS ARE THE **family** WE CHOOSE

One **friend** can change YOUR WHOLE **life**

LIFE IS **Better** WITH **friends**

friends MAKE THE WORLD A BETTER **place**

friendship IN ONE OF LIFE'S **greatest** TREASURES

Hard Times WILL ALWAYS **Reveal** TRUE **friends**

FRIENDSHIP IS NOT A BIG THING IT'S A **million** LITTLE THINGS

WE ARE BEST FRIEND

YOU'RE MY **Person**

I AM DEEPLY GRATEFUL FOR MY FRIENDS

FAMILY

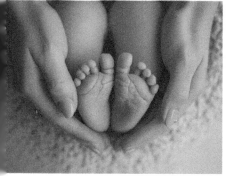

BLESS THE FOOD BEFORE US
The family BESIDE US
AND THE LOVE BETWEEN US

TOGETHER forever NEVER APART maybe in distance BUT NEVER in heart

WE MAY NOT HAVE IT ALL TOGETHER BUT TOGETHER WE HAVE IT ALL

Every FAMILY has a story WELCOME TO OURS

Family

SIDE BY SIDE OR MILES AWAY Family will always -BE- CONNECTED BY HEART

Family

this is us
OUR LIFE • OUR STORY • OUR HOME

Family IS A GIFT that lasts forever

WE ARE UNITED IN OUR LOVE FOR ONE ANOTHER

SELF-CARE is not SELFISH

SELFCARE

LOVE your self FIRST

WILL IT matter A YEAR from now?

REMEMBER that YOU ARE amazing

STOP DOUBTING yourself

SMILE BREATHE AND GO slowly

YOU'VE totally got this

self-care home spa

I ENJOY TAKING CARE OF MYSELF

MONEY
ISN'T EVERYTHING
BUT EVERYTHING
NEED **MONEY**

talk
BUSINESS
to me

but first
CASH

FINANCE

MASTER MONEY MANIFESTOR

Money is All I Need

Annual Savings: $1,500

Savings:

$1,500

1.000.000$

100.000$

10.000$

1.000$

MY SUCCESS IS INEVITABLE

MY SUCCESS IS INEVITABLE

WORKOUT

Fear IS A LIAR

EXCUSES DON'T BURN Calories

BE STRONGER THAN YOUR EXCUSES

Waiting on rest DAY

RUNNING LATE IS MY Cardio

GYM hair DON'T Care

Cardio IS hardio

WAKE UP BEAUTY IT'S TIME TO beast

EAT SLEEP
GYM
REPEAT

I Workout to
BURN
off the
CRAZY

EAT
SLEEP
gym
RepeaT

IT DOESN'T GET
EASIER
YOU JUST GET
STRONGER

THE BODY
ACHIEVES
WHAT THE
MIND
BELIEVES

GYM

Muscles
LOADING

PLEASE WAIT

I AM MOTIVATE, FIT & POWERFUL

Confident
&
Grateful

Beast
Mode
ON

Do All Thing
With
Love

Trust The
Process

MAKE
IT
HAPPEN

Passion +
Consistency
= Success

Make YOURSELF a priority

HEALTHY EATING

Eat HEALTHY live long LIVE Strong

Stay STRONG live LONG

a HEALTHY mind IN A HEALTHY BODY

ENERGIZE your LIFE

A healthy FUTURE begins now

Healthy food Healthy life

Health is Wealth

HEALTHY EATING

I EAT WELL AND FEEL GOOD IN MY BODY

BONUS ELEMENTS

EMBRACE THE JOY OF LIFE

WELCOME THE HAPPINESS THAT LIFE OFFERS

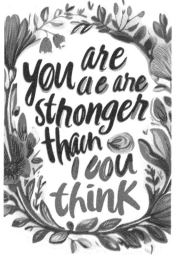

MOTIVATIONAL & INSPIRATIONAL

I AM MOTIVATED, CONSISTENT, AND DETERMINED

I AM MOTIVATED, CONSISTENT, AND DETERMINED

 LIVE PASSIONATELLY LOOVE DEEPLY

 STAY TRUE to YOURSELF

 COLLECT MOMENTS NOT THINGS

 BE KIND BE COURAGEOUS

 LIFE IS WHAT YOU MAKE

 DREAM BELIEVE ACHIEVE

I AM EXCITED FOR WHAT THE FUTURE HOLDS

 CHOOSE JOY EVERY DAY

 hello happiness

 SMILE OFTEN SPARKLE ALWAYS

 EMBRACE THE POSSIBILTIES

 TURN YOUR CAN'TS INTO CANS

Good things are Coming

POSITIVE vibes ONLY

Enjoy the little THINGS

FOCUS On the Good

YOU ARE capable worthy amazing

Perfectly Imperfect

I AM IN CONTROL OF MYSELF AND MY THOUGHTS

KILLIN' IT Every DAMN DAY

LOVE yourself

Be THE light MATTHEW 5:14

be kind

I AM enough

You Matter

I AM IN CONTROL OF MYSELF AND MY THOUGHTS

Happiness is a form of courage

enjoy the little things

Bloom where you are planted

you are AN AMAZING Human

BE kind ALWAYS

prove Them wrong

I AM ALIGNED WITH MY MISSION

MAKE someone SMILE today

Great things NEVER came from COMFORT zones

each DAY IS a new BEGINNING

If you can DREAM IT you can DO IT

Grow through what you go through

Adventures are the best way to learn

I AM ALIGNED WITH MY MISSION

IT'S TIME TO PLAN

Thank you!

We are thrilled to extend our heartfelt gratitude for your recent purchase of our **Vision Board Clip Art Book for 2025**. Your support means the world to us, and we can't wait for you to explore the creative possibilities that await within its pages.

We believe that creating a vision board is an incredible journey towards manifesting your dreams and goals. With this clip art book, we aimed to provide you with a toolkit to make that journey even more exciting and visually engaging. We trust that the vibrant illustrations and versatile elements will empower your vision board to truly reflect your aspirations.

As you dive into your creative projects, we kindly request your feedback. Your thoughts are invaluable to us and to others who are considering enhancing their creative process with our book. If you have a moment to spare, we would greatly appreciate it if you could share your experience and insights in a few words on Amazon. Your honest review will help fellow dreamers make informed decisions and discover the magic of our **Vision Board Clip Art Book.**

Wishing you endless inspiration and success as you craft your vision board masterpiece in 2025!

Warm regards,
Jasmine Eason

Made in the USA
Las Vegas, NV
17 December 2024

14734394R00044